T H E

TOP
500
POEMS

Other Columbia University Press Books

The Concise Columbia Book of Poetry.
William Harmon, ed. (1990)

The Columbia History of the American Novel.
Emory Elliott, ed. (1991)

Columbia Literary History of the United States.
Emory Elliott, ed. (1988)

The Columbia Granger's® Index to Poetry,
  Ninth Edition.
Edith P. Hazen and Deborah Fryer, eds. (1990)

The Columbia Granger's® Dictionary of
  Poetry Quotations.
Edith P. Hazen, ed. (1992)

The Columbia Granger's® Guide to
  Poetry Anthologies.
William Katz and Linda Sternberg Katz, eds. (1990)

The Concise Columbia Encyclopedia, Second Edition.
  (1989)

The Concise Columbia Dictionary of Quotations.
Robert Andrews, ed. (1990)

THE TOP 500 POEMS

**EDITED
BY
WILLIAM
HARMON**

A COLUMBIA ANTHOLOGY

COLUMBIA UNIVERSITY PRESS
New York

Columbia University Press wishes to express its
appreciation for assistance given by Corliss Lamont
toward the costs of publishing this book.

Columbia University Press
New York   Chichester, West Sussex
Copyright © 1992 Columbia University Press
All rights reserved

Library of Congress Cataloging-in-Publication Data
The Top 500 Poems / edited by William Harmon.
        p.   cm.
    ISBN 0-231-08028-X
    1. English poetry.   2. American poetry.
I. Harmon, William, 1938-
PR1175.C6417   1992
821.008—dc20   91-42239
                                                          CIP

⊗

Casebound editions of Columbia University Press
books are printed on permanent and durable acid-free
paper.

Printed in the United States of America

c   10   9   8   7   6   5   4

To
Caroline Ruth Harmon
for her third birthday

THE
TOP
500
POEMS

This Is *It!*

I am dedicating my thoughts in this book to my three-year-old daughter Caroline, because I have had her constantly in mind (and sometimes in lap) as I wrote about the poems collected here. Already, on a daily basis, she hears poetry, and before long she will be able to read it for herself. What general book of poetry should she, or anyone, start with? Well, this collection of the 500 poems that (according to *The Columbia Granger's*® *Index to Poetry*) have been anthologized most often impresses me as exactly the sort of book with which I would want to welcome her to the world of poetry in English. As a poet, teacher, editor, and father, I am satisfied that these 500 poems, with a bit of commentary, will serve as a splendid way for somebody to become acquainted with the best that has been written in the shorter poetic forms for about 750 years. As I have said to myself repeatedly, this is *it!*

This is the story of poetry in English, starting in the Middle Ages in England and ending in the English-speaking world of today. It starts with poems of a simplicity of form and directness of emotion that appeal instantly to children and adults alike. But mature artistry is on display from the beginning, as is that necessary preoccupation of maturity—time. Growing children are the most vivid reminders of our own aging, and this book demonstrates, from the beginning, that English poets have been obsessed with the passage of time. Much poetry seems to be aware of its situation in time and of its relation to the metronome, the clock, and the calendar. Among the earliest poems in this book there is a sense of seasons being born:

> Sumer is icumen in . . . .

> When April with its sweet showers . . . .

The season or month is there to be felt; the day is there to be seized. Poetry keeps telling us what happens in time. Poems beginning

"When" are much more numerous than those beginning "Where" or "If." As the meter is running, the recurrent message tapped out by the passing of measured time is mortality. (This undercurrent may account for the melancholy and fright that turn up even in lullabies and nursery rhymes, which suggest that life is an affair of breaking boughs, falling cradles, bridges falling down, falling down, falling down.)

But generally it has occurred to me, as I thought about these 500 poems, that English-speaking people have produced one of the greatest bodies of literature the world has ever seen. The drama has been a scene of brilliance since 1590; the novel is about a century younger. In poetry, however, the English genius goes right back into the Middle Ages. Great poetry has been written in the English language for at least 600 years. Dull periods have come along from time to time, true, but in most periods since Chaucer, who died in 1400, the English language has served somebody somewhere as the instrument of breathtaking poetry: epic, dramatic, lyric, satiric, meditative, nonsensical, as well as every conceivable combination and permutation.

The greatness of English poetry in a large way reflects on the peoples who have spoken English, their culture, weather, humor, even their "character," whatever that term may suggest. They have liked songs and stories, and they have believed in talk, all the way from tavern conversation to parliamentary debate.

And they have had the English language itself. Modern English, the language in which my daughter is even now gaining fluency, incorporates Indo-European elements from northwestern and southwestern Europe—from Anglo-Saxon (Germanic) and French (Italic). Because of its history, English has become, in respect of vocabulary and syntax, practically a double language, commonly offering speakers a number of different ways of saying something. For the sake of the arts of poetry, several features of the peculiarly English language-mixture have been inexhaustibly useful. The large vocabulary furnishes a broad range of possibilities with much opportunity for nuances and ironies of meaning along with complex harmonies and textures. Some poets have favored the Germanic extreme of substantial syllables that stay close to the earth and move rather slowly, as in Hopkins's "Inversnaid":